Little Acts of

Kindness

COUNTLESS WAYS TO
BRIGHTEN SOMEONE'S DAY

This edition published in 2019
By SJG Publishing, HP22 6NF, UK

Author: Rebecca Dickinson
Cover design: Milestone Creative
Contents design: seagulls.net

ISBN: 978-1-911517-71-9

Printed in China

10 9 8 7 6 5 4 3 2 1

'A little thought and a little kindness are often worth more than a great deal of money.'

John Ruskin

Introduction

Never has there been a better or more important time to be kind. In a world that feels polluted by fear and hate, a world in which communities are breaking down and social media is replacing social interaction, there has never been a more urgent need for kindness.

In a world in which one in four people experience a mental health problem and many more are lonely and displaced, it's the little acts of kindness that make a difference.

Knowing that you've touched someone's life, even in a small way, provides an enormous feeling of fulfilment. Research shows that acts of kindness don't just enhance the lives of others, they are good for our own wellbeing too, boosting health, happiness and even life expectancy.

'Wherever there is a human being, there is an opportunity for kindness.'

Seneca

Kind actions increase our feelings of confidence, worth and compassion. This, in turn, makes us more likeable and trustworthy and therefore more likely to receive acts of kindness ourselves.

What's more, when you do something kind it causes your brain to release extra dopamine, the chemical that gives us a natural high. In short, kindness isn't just good for others, it's good for you, too.

This book is packed with suggested acts of kindness to carry out, along with inspiring quotations. The suggestions range from the very small to the undeniably huge, but all have the power to make a difference. Why don't you keep a journal to note your own acts and their outcome, to help you become the person you always wanted to be?'

LITTLE ACTS OF KINDNESS TO

Strangers

Baby steps of kindness can help us to feel
more connected to the world in which we live
and the people with whom we share it.

There's also something addictive
about kindness. The more good you do,
the better you feel, creating a cycle of
positive reinforcement. This spurs you on
to do more good, until those baby steps
become big, confident strides.

Two Minute Acts
OF KINDNESS

- Pick up litter instead of just walking past – extra points if you can pick up dog poo.

- Clear your own table in a cafe or coffee shop.

- Give some change to a busker and stop to listen to them for a couple of minutes.

- Ask someone who looks lost if they need directions.

- Wipe down gym equipment after you've used it.

- Leave public toilets as you'd wish to find them.

'No act of kindness, however small, is ever wasted.'

Aesop

THIRTY MINUTE ACTS OF KINDNESS

Taking half an hour out of our own lives now and then could make someone else's whole day. If thirty minutes feels unattainable, perhaps have a look at how much time you spend on social media, or watching television, and see if you can make a time-swap.

- Have a clear-out and take clothes and other items you haven't used in a while to a charity shop, instead of hanging on to them 'just in case'.

- Leave larger items outside your home with a sign saying 'free to whoever needs it.'

- Make a care package for someone.

- Pot up plants and seedlings and give them away.

- Tidy an elderly person's garden or mow their lawn.

- Ask someone who's waiting for a taxi if they'd like a free lift, then take them to their destination.

Little Acts

OF REGULAR KINDNESS

If you're studying hard for exams, working all hours, running around after small children, or caring for elderly or poorly relatives, you may not be in a position to commit to a weekly act of kindness. Don't worry; your time will come. However, if you are in a position to offer a regular commitment here are some things you could try.

- Volunteer for a charity.

- Help out at local groups such as playgroups, sports clubs, or scout groups.

- Offer your services at local events like fundraisers and school fairs.

- Find out about visiting or writing to people in prison.

- 'Adopt' an elderly person in your neighborhood.

- Start a weekly newspaper discussion group in your local library, to bring people together.

- Set up a monthly book group in your home, or a hall.

'As you grow older, you will discover that you have two hands, one for helping yourself, the other for helping others.'

Audrey Hepburn

LITTLE ACTS OF ANONYMOUS KINDNESS

Perhaps the greatest acts of kindness are those which are done in secret and for which we will never be thanked.

- Take beautiful flowers to your local hospital and ask staff to pass them on to someone whose bedside table is empty. Include a note wishing them well.

- Tape a few coins to a vending machine for someone to discover.

- Leave some sanitary items in a public toilet with a note saying they are for anyone who needs them.

- Pay the bill of the person behind you in the drive-thru and ask the cashier to pass on a note saying 'you've just been gifted.'

- Go to justgiving.com and find a story that touches your heart. Then leave an anonymous donation for someone you've never met.

'No kind action ever stops with itself. One kind action leads to another. Good example is followed. A single act of kindness throws out roots in all directions, and the roots spring up and make new trees. The greatest work that kindness does to others is that it makes them kind themselves.'

Amelia Earhart

Little Acts

OF UNEXPECTED KINDNESS

- Add an extra item to the end of your food shop, such a cake or small box of chocolates, as a gift for the cashier who's had a long day.

'We don't have to engage in grand, heroic actions to participate in the process of change. Small acts, when multiplied by millions of people, can transform the world.'

Howard Zinn

Why not start a 'kindness journal'? Take a notebook in which to note down your acts of kindness, along with the reactions you receive. Don't be deterred if some people are wary or suspicious – it may be that they are just unaccustomed to kindness.

- Buy a box of ice creams and hand them out to strangers on a hot day.

- Take a box of donuts to your local fire or ambulance station, with a note of thanks.

- Buy lunch, or coffee, for a homeless person.

- Write inspiring messages on postcards and hand them out during rush hour.

- Take an extra large umbrella out on a rainy day and offer to share it with someone who doesn't have one.

- Buy a parking ticket for longer than you need and pass it on to someone else when you leave.

LITTLE ACTS OF KINDNESS

Just For Fun

Kindness is serious, but that doesn't mean it can't be enjoyable, too...

- Attach a swing to a tree in an area where children play and leave it there for them to enjoy.

- Plant bulbs in unloved patches of earth.

- Plant a fruit tree in a public place, as long as it doesn't disturb other plants.

- Pull up weeds from planted borders.

- If you grow your own fruit or veg and have a glut, leave the surplus outside your home, or outside a school, with a sign saying 'please help yourself.'

- Leave a small amount of money in an envelope and hide it somewhere for someone to find, with a note inviting them to spend it on someone else, or on themselves if they need to.

- Leave a jar of honey on someone's doorstep with a note saying 'a gift from the bees.'

- Leave fresh eggs with a note saying 'a gift from the hens.'

- Leave a magazine on a public bench (as long as it's not raining.)

- Join the pebble painting movement – you don't need to be an artist, you could paint a rainbow, an animal, a cartoon character or just a pattern on your pebble. Include a heart-warming message like 'kindness matters' or 'love rocks' then leave it somewhere, such as alongside a path or in a woodland, to be discovered. The idea is that someone will pick it up and a feel a connection to another human being. They can then keep the pebble or move it somewhere else, and share on social media to spread the kindness message.

LITTLE ACTS OF KINDNESS TO

Friends, Loved Ones & Acquaintances

LITTLE ACTS OF TLC

We don't have to spend money to be kind. Often, our most precious resources are our time and attention.

- Offer to give a friend or relative a makeover, or manicure.

- Offer to wash, dry and style someone's hair for them.

- Give someone who's feeling stressed a head massage – and feel their tension drain away.

- Give someone a neck and shoulder rub – you don't need to be an expert, anyone can do this.

- Wash a tired friend or family member's feet, apply beautifully scented cream and give them a pedicure.

- Babysit for a parent you know who needs a night out, or an afternoon to themselves.

> Why not make a list of all the people you know who could use a little TLC right now, then come up with a plan to show them that you care?

Little Acts of PLC

(PRACTICAL LOVING CARE)

- Cook a healthy meal for someone who's recently had a baby, or been unwell.

- Offer to take someone's laundry, then bring it back clean and folded.

'If you want others to be happy, practice compassion. If you want to be happy, practice compassion.'

Dalai Lama

> Make a list of all the people who could use some practical help right now and try to think about ways in which you could make a difference.

- Make freezer meals for someone who doesn't have family close by. Better still, invite them over for dinner.

- Clean someone else's bathroom, or kitchen.

- Do a neighbor's shopping.

- Walk a busy person's dog.

- Give someone a lift – even if it's out of your way.

- Offer to take on some of the workload of a colleague who's overstretched. If it's not your level of expertise, fetch them a coffee and offer moral support instead.

YOU'VE GOT
(Snail) Mail!

Everyone loves receiving things in the mail! No, not those ominous brown envelopes. But wonderful, unexpected tokens of kindness. Surprise your friends and family by sending fun and thoughtful gifts for no reason at all. Here are some things that fit perfectly inside an envelope.

- A packet of sunflower seeds.

- A sheet of stickers.

- A special photograph.

- A poem you've written out, or written yourself!

- Popping candy.

- A child's artwork.

- A packet of hot chocolate.

- A face mask.

- A mini packet of jelly beans.

True kindness
is doing something
and not expecting
anything in return.

SHARE THE THINGS

You Love

When you give someone a gift from your heart, you give them a little piece of yourself.

- Make a playlist for someone who needs more music in their life.

- Pass on a favorite book with a personal recommendation. Most of us rarely read books more than once anyway, so resist the urge to hang on to books as decoration, and spread the joy of reading.

- Donate magazines you've finished with to others who'll enjoy them.

- Loan someone your bike (or let them keep it if you don't use it yourself.)

24

- If you have a pet, offer to loan him or her out to an animal lover who's not in a position to have a pet of their own. Animals are great therapy.

- The next time somebody says how much they love something you own, such as a pretty vase or an item of clothing, hand it to them and tell them you'd love them to have it.

'What I call the depth of generosity is when people are very fond of giving away what they need most themselves.'

Oscar Wilde

BE A CHEERLEADER

You don't need to join a squad, learn a chant, or dress in lycra, but if you know someone who's taking part in an event, whether it's their first ever parkrun, or a full blown marathon or triathlon, turn out to cheer them on. You could make banners or flags to wave, or design printed T-shirts to wear for the occasion.

Your cheering will really spur them on and could even help them cross the finish line with a personal best. And if they're running for a good cause, your support will mean even more.

Or perhaps you have a friend or relative who is appearing on stage. Buy front row tickets for the first night to let them know you're rooting for them. And be the loudest clapper!

'Never discourage anyone who continually makes progress, no matter how slow.'

Plato

GIVE AWAY
YOUR SKILLS

For Free

Whatever you're good at, whether it's gardening, baking, spelling, knitting, decorating, massage, or fixing cars or computers, why not use your skills to help others?

Little Ways

TO PUT YOUR PASSION AND EXPERTISE TO GOOD USE

- Great with animals – volunteer in a rescue center.

- Computer whizz – give a tutorial to an older person who feels left behind. Set them up with an email account if they don't have one, or show them how to do online shopping.

- Confident driver – help someone who's less confident to feel safe behind the wheel again. Perhaps they've had a break from driving due to illness or circumstance and need someone to accompany them until they feel ready to drive alone again.

- **Strong swimmer** – offer to teach a friend who's never had lessons how to swim. Stick with it until they've conquered 50m.

- **Have a natural affinity with children** – volunteer in a school, or even look into fostering.

- **Website guru** – help someone with a small business to get online, or help a would-be blogger get started.

'The end result of kindness is that it draws people to you.'

Anita Roddick

TEACH CHILDREN

To Be Kind

Kind children become kind adults, paving the way for a kind future. What's more, children learn by example, so the best way to encourage children to be kind is to model kindness yourself.

It doesn't matter whether they are your own children, nieces, nephews, friends' or neighbors' children. You don't need to be a parent to be a good influence – the way you act in front of children will shape the way they act towards others.

- Model politeness and good manners such as 'please' and 'thank you.'

- Give equal respect to everyone you come into contact with, whether they are cleaners or doctors.

- Avoid speaking badly about people.

- Avoid chiding children for mistakes, but encourage them to try again.

- Give children your undiluted attention rather than being distracted by phones or other adults, so they feel valued and learn to value others.

- Play – children learn best through play. It also helps them to develop qualities of turn-taking, fairness, being a good sport and teamwork.

'What wisdom can you find that is greater than kindness?'

Jean Jacques Rousseau

MORE WAYS TO FOSTER KINDNESS IN CHILDREN

- Share books with kind themes – this is great for bonding as well as building empathy.

- Stress the importance of having 'kind hands' – hands that are gentle and don't hurt other people or animals, or plants.

- Talk to children about people in the world who are less fortunate than they are, to encourage empathy and teach the importance of sharing.

- Involve them in your own acts of kindness, so they discover that helping feels good as well as doing good.

- Ask children to help out around the house with age-appropriate tasks and praise them when they do so. Kindness starts at home!

- Talk to them about the importance of being a great friend and always looking out for others at school.

LITTLE ACTS OF KINDNESS TOWARDS ELDERLY PEOPLE

Older people are just people who have been alive longer than the rest of us. They have the same needs for friendship, happiness, kindness and fun as everyone else.

But sadly, many elderly people, especially those with health and mobility issues, end their lives in dreadful loneliness and isolation.

Being kind to elderly people means checking they're ok and offering companionship. It's about finding a moment to make a small difference and brighten their day. The great thing is it will probably brighten your day too.

What's more, older people come with decades of experience. Whether it's marriage, friendship, work, children or sex, the chances are they've been there, done that; so don't be afraid to look beyond the wrinkles and consult their wisdom.

ACTIVITIES TO ENJOY WITH

Older People

- **Interview them** – older people are living history books. Ask them to share stories and talk about a specific time in their lives. The chances are you'll be amazed at what you discover. Ask if you can record their memories to preserve for the future.

- **Read out loud** – everyone loves listening to stories and for people with poor eyesight, this can be a real treat. Choose a book or articles that you'll both enjoy.

- **Play games** – if a run in the park isn't an option, suggest dominoes or cards or do a puzzle together.

'People will never forget how you made them feel.'

Maya Angelou

- **Bring the kids over** – older people often love young faces and there's nothing like the sound of children laughing to inject a bit of happiness.

- **Set up a bird feeder** – if an elderly relative or neighbor is unable to get out much, bring the wildlife to their window instead.

- **Hold their hand** – older people have the same need for touch as younger people and the simple act of taking their hand in yours provides a vital sense of connection.

Little Acts

OF KINDNESS FOR PEOPLE WITH CANCER AND OTHER ILLNESSES

A cancer diagnosis, whatever the prognosis, is always a life-changing event. The fact that it is incredibly common doesn't make it any easier. While we may not be able to help on a medical level, simple human kindness can make a world of difference to how someone feels and copes with treatment.

• Practical support – cancer can turn your life upside down. Offering to help out with the day-to-day stuff like doing the school run, looking after pets and watering plants means less for the sufferer to worry about.

- **Emotional support** – be there with hugs, tissues, compassion and gentle reassurance.

- **Financial support** – from hospital parking fees to not being able to work, cancer can take a huge financial toll on sufferers and their families. If you can't afford to chip in yourself, consider holding a fundraising event.

- **Support for carers** – caring for someone with cancer is tough, too. So offer to give carers a break by taking over for a bit, or just let them offload their own worries.

'The best
things in life
aren't things.'

Art Buchwald

'The smallest act of kindness is worth more than the grandest intention.'

Oscar Wilde.

THOUGHTFUL GIFT IDEAS FOR

Cancer Patients

The best thing you can give someone who has been diagnosed with cancer is your time and your love. But if you want to express kindness in other ways too, here are some suggestions. Of course, you could adapt these for people suffering from other illness as well.

- A silk pillow case – hair loss can be physically as well as emotionally painful. The scalp can feel extremely tender and cotton pillow cases can make this worse, whereas silk ones don't feel like they are pulling.

- A supportive pillow – for resting the neck, back or arm during treatment sessions.

- Ginger tea – to help with the nausea caused by treatment.

- A guardian angel figurine – to hang up or keep to hand for reassurance and to remind them that you are there in thought.

- A craft kit – to fill the time. Cancer involves lots of waiting. Not crafty? Try sudoku or word games.

- A pamper or reflexology session – for when they're feeling up to it, or to look forward to after treatment.

- A chemo quilt – ask a group of friends to make one square each – for example knitted squares, or pieces of fabric taken from clothing. Get everyone to write messages of hope and encouragement on the squares using a marker pen, then put them all together to make a patchwork of kindness.

- Organic hand cream or moisturiser – to counteract the dryness caused by treatment.

- Audio books – for when they don't feel up to reading.

- Slippers – ideal for hospital stays and not just for Christmas!

- Soft hats and scarves – instead of a wig, or for when they don't feel like wearing one.

- A collection of inspirational verses or sayings – even more meaningful if you can write them out yourself.

- An adult coloring book – coloring is no longer just for kids! There are now hundreds of beautiful coloring books for adults which can help with mindfulness and relaxation. Don't forget to buy some pens, too.

- A visit from a favorite celebrity – ok, this one might take a bit of work, but just think of the reaction! If a visit is out of the question, request a personal message instead.

LITTLE ACTS OF KINDNESS THAT

Push our Comfort Zones

BECOME AN ORGAN DONOR

Registering to donate your organs in the event of your death could be the most worthwhile act of your life. Tragically, people die every day while waiting for an organ transplant. So register now, if you haven't done so already.

The majority of people say that they would be willing to donate their organs after their death but unfortunately many people don't get round to recording this decision. (Some countries now have an 'opt-out' system where it's assumed you would be a donor unless you actively register your decision to 'opt out'.)

If you do sign up to become an organ donor make sure you tell your family too, as they will need to give their consent in the event of your death. Families who agree to donation say it helps with their grief and that they feel an enormous sense of pride at knowing their relative gave others the chance of a new beginning.

BECOME A

Living Donor

You don't need to wait until death to help others with your body. There are plenty of things you can give while you are alive, too.

- Blood – giving blood is simple and safe and could save a life, so close this book for a minute and register now!

- Other blood products – if you are already a blood donor, you could consider donating platelets and plasma, or even bone marrow.

- Hair – if you have long hair and feel like a change, why not have it chopped for a charity that makes wigs for cancer patients? It could make a world of difference to how a sufferer feels about themselves during treatment.

- A kidney or part of your liver – you can donate these and still live a perfectly healthy life.

- Breastmilk – if you're a nursing mother with milk to spare, ask your nearest neonatal unit if they have a milk bank. Donor breast milk can make a huge difference to premature or poorly babies, whose own mothers aren't able to provide it, as it's more easily digested than formula milk and helps protect against infections.

'Where it is not possible for the biological mother to breast feed, the first alternative, if available, should be the use of human breast milk from other sources.' (statement by WHO/UNICEF)

'Kind words can be short and easy to speak but their echoes are truly endless.'

Mother Teresa

Speak kindly...

It's easy to speak kindly to people we like, but it can be tempting to snap at people who get on our nerves: the cold-caller, the door-to-door salesperson, the parking inspector. Yet there's a good chance they dislike their job as much as you dislike being on the receiving end. So the next time you encounter someone who tests your patience, remember they're human too, and surprise them by speaking kindly.

What's more, it will make you feel better, too. Arguments only lead to feelings of anger and negativity on both sides, whereas gentleness benefits everyone.

...EVEN WHEN YOU

Disagree

You don't have to agree with someone to be nice to them. Make it clear it's their politics or their beliefs you disagree with and try to engage in a reasoned, calm conversation instead.

Question your long-held opinions, too, and open your mind to different ways of thinking. Be humble enough to change your mind if you discover your own arguments are flawed.

Even if your opponent's views are clearly wrong or unfounded, refrain from anger; you're more likely to sway their opinions through peaceful discussion, rather than shouting or slamming their beliefs. And remember, kindness is never wrong.

BE GENTLE

Kindness is not a weakness. In a dog-eat-dog world, it can sometimes appear that the only way to be successful, or to convince others of your point of view, is to trample on anyone who gets in the way, or bully them into submission, like a shouty politician or a ruthless business person.

Yet it's possible, and far more admirable, to be both strong and kind. Shouting only instils fear and resentment, yet truly successful people get others on side through warmth, friendship, honesty and gentle persuasion.

'Forget injuries; never forget kindness.'

Confucius

SPEAK IN TONGUES!

If you live in a multicultural neighborhood or come into contact with people of different races and religions at work, school, or college, try to learn a few simple words and phrases such as 'hello,' 'welcome' and 'how are you?' in different languages. Then make an effort to greet people in their native tongues as an expression of inclusivity.

'Kind hearts are the gardens. Kind thoughts are the roots. Kind words are the blossoms. Kind deeds are the fruits.'

Kirpal Singh

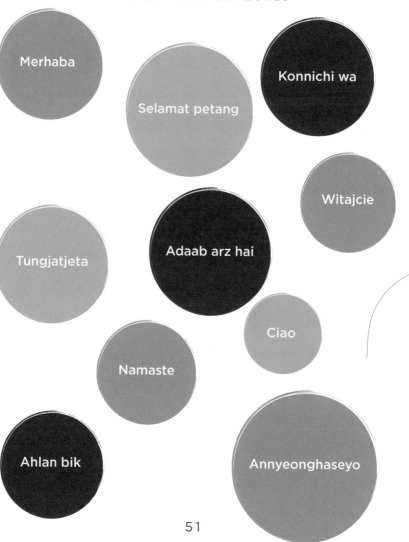

Merhaba

Konnichi wa

Selamat petang

Witajcie

Tungjatjeta

Adaab arz hai

Ciao

Namaste

Ahlan bik

Annyeonghaseyo

Embrace Diversity

Once you've got past 'hello' make an effort to get to know people from different cultures, races, religions, or sexual orientations, on a deeper level.

Learning about the different ways of life of people from a multitude of backgrounds promotes empathy and builds bridges of kindness between communities. Getting to know people from different cultures can also provide a fascinating insight into the customs, foods and traditions of other countries. What's more, the chances are you will also realize how much you have in common with people from other cultures.

'No one is born hating another person...People must learn to hate, and if they can learn to hate, they can be taught to love, for love comes more naturally to the human heart than its opposite.'

Nelson Mandela

'Kindness is a language which the deaf can hear and the blind can see.'

Mark Twain

MORE WAYS TO PROMOTE CROSS-CULTURAL KINDNESS

• Campaign on behalf of refugees, victims of war and other vulnerable groups.

• Support causes that support the rights of people from different backgrounds.

• Stand up to or report any incidents of racism or other forms of discrimination you witness online or elsewhere.

• Take time to give simple explanations to people who are still getting to grips with English. Help them to fill in forms.

• Read books written by or about people from different backgrounds.

• Take notice of what's going on in the world by reading newspapers and listening to the news.

LITTLE ACTS OF

Financial Kindness

Kindness doesn't have to cost a penny, but
if you're fortunate enough to have more
than you need, here are some alternatives to
stashing it all away in a savings account.

- Donate a small percentage of your income to a worthwhile cause. If you set up a direct debit you won't even notice it coming out each month.

- Sponsor a child in a developing country.

- Start a coin jar, and use it to store loose change. When the jar is full, empty it into a charity collection.

- Sponsor your friends. Or if you can't afford a donation, help them out by sharing fundraising posts on social media.

- Leave tips.

- If you're not in a position to give financially at the moment, promise yourself you will when you're better off.

- Leave a gift to charity in your will.

'No one has ever become poor by giving,'

Anne Frank

'Great opportunities to help others seldom come, but small ones surround us every day.'

Sally Koch

SHOP KINDLY

Whether it's food, clothing, furniture, electrical appliances or other gadgets, many of us buy way more than we really need, which only fuels the problem of waste and causes us to overspend.

By rethinking our shopping habits, we can save money while reducing our impact on the environment.

- Make do and mend – whether it's fixing a puncture or sewing up a hole in a T-shirt, it's amazing how many things can be repaired. If you don't know how to do it, just look on YouTube!

- Borrow and lend – instead of splashing out on an item you'll only use once, such as a laminator for a one-off project, see if you can borrow instead. Loan your own stuff out, too.

- Avoid throwaway items – look for items that are designed to last, rather than designed for landfill.

LITTLE CHANGES, BIG DIFFERENCE

Try making some of these small adjustments to your shopping cart to increase your kindness footprint.

- Look for fair trade products which ensure people are paid fairly for their labor.

- Avoid items with excessive or non-recyclable packaging and unnecessary plastic.

- Support local and small businesses by using independent stores.

- Only buy groceries you really need. The same goes for non-food items like electrical appliances, clothing and toys which all contribute to the problem of landfill.

- Recycle and reuse whenever possible.

- Sign up for loyalty cards and use the rewards on other people.

DON'T BE SUCKED IN
BY THE SALES

In our consumerist culture there is the constant urge to spend, spend, spend. We are bombarded with relentless incentives to buy: Black Friday, end-of-season sales, and a carousel of special offers and promotions, all designed to make us feel like we are missing out if we don't part with our cash.

Media images of people who line up all night to get their hands on the latest phone, scenes of people elbowing each other out of the way to grab a bargain, paint a sad image of modern society.

The next time a sale comes to town, ask yourself if you really need a new TV, or those shoes, or the latest bag in this year's 'must-have' color.

Unless you genuinely need something, avoid the temptation to buy just because there's a sale on. Remember, there will always be another sale. And another!

Shop AND Drop

Think how lovely it would be if every time we went shopping we got into the habit of throwing in an extra item for someone in need. A bottle of juice or a pair of socks for a homeless person, tins of beans for a soup kitchen or food bank, a bunch of flowers for someone who's feeling down. Even when our own finances are tight, there are often ways we can squeeze in an extra item for someone else.

- Look out for offers like BOGOF and give the 'free' item away.

- Instead of buying single items, buy multipacks – which usually work out cheaper anyway – and donate anything you can spare to someone in need.

- Exchange branded products for cheaper versions and use the money you save to buy something useful for someone else.

- Swap the bar of chocolate you don't really need for a bar of soap for someone who needs one but has no means of buying one.

'A kind and compassionate act is often its own reward.'

William John Bennett

'May I never get too busy in my own affairs that I fail to respond to the needs of others with kindness and compassion.'

Thomas Jefferson

HANG ON TO THE RECEIPT

The next time you do a weekly shop, keep the receipt, then grab a pen. Now try the following:

- Cross out any items you could do without – it could be a packet of cookies, a bottle of wine, or half the fridge. Add these savings together.

- Now underline all the branded, or top of the range items. Could you swap these for cheaper versions? Work out, or estimate, how much you'd save.

- Now cross out anything you often end up throwing away. It could be a couple of bananas, or the loaf of bread that usually goes mouldy. Be honest! Work out how much you spend on food that goes in the bin.

- Add the last three amounts together, then subtract that sum from the total on the receipt. How much could you save per week?

- Could you do something positive with the change?

TRY A LITTLE

Experiment

Could you go without food for a week?

No, this isn't a call to starvation! But a fun exercise to see if you can live on nothing but store cupboard ingredients for seven days: the chickpeas that have been there for years, the half-finished bag of rice, that health product you bought on a whim, but never got round to eating, the herbs and spices that are probably way past their best before dates.

Try not to cheat, but obviously don't make yourself ill! And make sure children don't miss out on vital nutrition.

As well as being a chance to get creative and use your imagination in the kitchen, this is also a great way of using up food that might otherwise get thrown out.

But most importantly, it encourages us to think about what it's like for people who really don't have enough to eat. If you have children, encourage them to join in too and talk about food poverty together as a way of encouraging empathy.

At the end of the week, you might want to donate the money you've saved by not buying any groceries to a hunger charity.

'Generosity is giving more than you can.'

Khalil Gibran

LITTLE ACTS OF

Online Kindness

LEAVE A COMMENT – AND BE NICE!

You only have to read the comments section of an online newspaper article to witness the level of hatred that festers on the internet.

Such sections can be a magnet for unkindness and are awash with snide remarks and negativity. Even websites that are supposed to be supportive online communities can often attract hurtful comments.

The next time you enjoy reading an article or agree with something that's written, take a moment to say so. It's so easy for people to sit behind a computer screen being spiteful. But a couple of lines of kindness is all it takes to put a different spin on things. So write something nice – you never know who might feel better for reading it.

'When you are kind to others, it not only changes you, it changes the world.'

Harold Kushner

POST POSITIVE REVIEWS

If you've had a great experience, don't be shy! A positive review lets other people know about something you've enjoyed and lets the person responsible know they're doing a good job.

- Write a review of a book you've read and loved – top marks if you also offer to pass the book on!

- Leave a glowing report on trip advisor.

- Give an online seller a positive rating.

- Recommend a restaurant and something on the menu.

- Post a friendly comment on a website or blog.

- Support small businesses by following their Facebook page, Twitter or Instagram accounts.

- If you haven't had a positive experience, don't shout about it online but contact the organization, or person responsible, directly.

'Be kind whenever possible.

It is always possible.'

Dalai Lama

'The world is changed by your example, not by your opinion.'

Paulo Coelho

USE SOCIAL MEDIA TO BRING PEOPLE TOGETHER

Counteract the isolation caused by social media, by using it to unite communities.

- Set up a WhatsApp group for your street to foster community spirit and provide a place where people can ask for help. Although don't use it as a substitute for knocking on people's doors!

- Start a Facebook group for a school, club or organisation to which you belong, to provide information and create a sense of pride.

- Use Twitter, Facebook and Instagram to promote local businesses and events.

- Give away things you don't need on community pages. When someone comes round to collect something, invite them in for a cuppa, as long as you feel it's safe to do so.

Cyberkindness

- Share videos that make people laugh or smile – we all need to watch babies being cute and cats falling into toilets!

- Help raise awareness of important issues by sharing calls to action.

- Celebrate friends' good news by 'liking' their posts and sending them congratulations.

- Share or retweet posts from people asking for help or information.

- Treat people on the internet in the same way as you would treat them in real life. If you want to express a different opinion, do so respectfully. Encourage others to do the same.

- Avoid websites where people can remain anonymous. Anonymity features can be used to harass people.

- If you're a parent, don't allow under-aged children to have their own social media accounts.

- If you have teenagers with social media accounts, protect them by knowing their passwords and monitoring posts, so you can keep an eye out for potential bullying and other issues.

- Restrict screen time for children of all ages and encourage them to do other activities besides.

'Where is the wisdom we have lost in knowledge? Where is the knowledge we have lost in infomation?'

TS Elliot

LITTLE ACTS OF

Environmental Kindness

When we treat the Earth with kindness and respect we are preserving it for our children and future generations, so ultimately we are being kind to humans, too.

Yet climate change, pollution, extinction and the depletion of fossil fuels are all mounting threats to the planet and its inhabitants.

It's heartbreaking to watch communities devastated by increasingly common 'freak' weather events, to see videos of birds choking on plastic, or oceans spewing out sewage, or to learn that the last male white rhino has died, or to learn that bee populations are dwindling thanks to unnecessary chemicals.

Yet by changing our own lives and using resources kindly we can all make a difference – and together that difference can be global.

'We won't have a society if we destroy the environment.'

Margaret Mead

SHOUT
About it!

Kindness doesn't normally involve shouting, but there are exceptions. Awareness is vital when it comes to protecting the planet and ensuring its future survival.

There is an urgent need for action, and we can do this by supporting environmental campaigns, and by lobbying politicians and businesses to take responsibility, reduce waste and cut emissions.

We can also help raise public awareness by sharing information and encouraging others to take part in events such as: beach cleans, litter picks, street cleans and meat-free days, and of course by setting our own examples.

Try to make the acts on the next few pages part of your environmentally friendly lifestyle.

Wildlife

BEETLES, BUGS AND BUTTERFLIES GALORE

- Avoid using chemicals like pesticides and weedkillers in your garden, which harm wildlife and the soil.

- Feed the birds and create a bird bath in summer (but not if you have a cat!)

- Create a 'bug house' to attract insects.

- Teach children the names of flowers, plants and mini-beasts so that they grow up caring about the natural world and its survival.

Animals

ALL CREATURES GREAT AND SMALL

- If you eat meat, dairy and eggs, try to buy free range and organic rather than mass-farmed products.

- Only eat fish from sustainable sources.

- Support conservation projects.

- If you are looking to get a pet, go to rescue centers rather than pet shops and animal breeders.

- 'Adopt' an endangered animal.

- Choose cosmetics and other products that haven't been tested on animals.

- Treat pets and other animals with the same kindness you would treat a human.

- Slow down – many wild animals are killed by speeding motorists.

'The animals of the world exist for their own reasons. They were not made for humans any more than black people were made for white, or women created for men.'

Alice Walker

Pollution

AND THE ENVIRONMENT

Take care of the land and the land will take care of you.

- Walk or cycle, rather than driving. It's better for you, too!

- If walking isn't an option, use public transport when possible.

- If you really need to drive, car-share.

- Enjoy the countryside, but leave nothing but footprints and take nothing but photographs.

- Every time you go out, make an effort to pick up at least three pieces of litter. Imagine how clean the world would be if everyone did this!

- Recycle, recycle, recycle.

Food

THINK NEED, NOT GREED

- Start a compost pile for food waste, or get a compost bin. You'll have the added bonus of free nutrients for your soil, too.

- Use or freeze leftovers.

- Don't get too hung up on best before dates – food is often perfectly ok after the date on the package.

- Set aside a day, or days, each week to go meat-free – top marks if you can go vegan.

- Buy organically produced foods when possible and if you can afford to.

- Grow some of your own food to reduce reliance on commercial farming and decrease your carbon footprint. You don't need a large garden, even a few containers can make a difference.

'There is a sufficiency in the world for man's need but not for man's greed.'

Mahatma Gandhi

Water

So freely available to some, yet so desperately needed by others.

- Drink tap rather than bottled water.

- Reuse household water from washing and cooking for watering plants.

- Collect rainwater in containers outside to use in the garden.

- Take showers rather than baths. Or share the tub!

- Water the garden first thing in the morning or last thing in the evening to reduce loss from evaporation.

- Fix leaky taps.

- Turn off the tap while you're brushing your teeth and teach children to do the same.

Energy

There's no need to revert to candles and horse-power to reduce our energy consumption. Try these ideas instead.

- Turn off computers and other electrical items at night and when not in use.

- Turn down the heating or air conditioning by a notch or two.

- Hang washing out to dry instead of using a tumble drier.

- Switch to energy-saving light bulbs.

Choose energy-efficient washing machines and other appliances.

Maximize your oven – if you're cooking a meal, why not knock up a cake, or something else at the same time?

Put lids on pans when cooking to conserve heat.

Don't fill the kettle, only boil the amount you need.

'We do not inherit the Earth from our ancestors, we borrow it from our children.'

Native American proverb

'If you are not a part of the solution, you are a part of the problem.'

Eldridge Cleaver

PLASTICS

Plastic is taking over our world and our oceans. Here are some items it's kinder to go without.

- Straws – mouths are back in fashion!

- Takeaway cups – invest in a reusable one.

- Carrier bags – take cloth bags whenever you go shopping and keep a stash in the car, too.

- Microplastics – avoid cosmetics like face scrubs which frequently contain these.

- Coffee capsules – use a stove pot or cafetiere instead.

- Razors – buy metal or reusable ones. Or go hairy or bearded!

- Liquid soap – opt for bars of soap instead of shower gels and liquid hand soaps. They last longer, too.

- Plastic toys in Happy Meals (if you really want to order a Happy Meal, ask them to leave out the toy.)

FINAL LITTLE ACTS OF KINDNESS FOR

Special Occasions

HAPPIER BIRTHDAY!

If you can't think of anything you really want for your next birthday (or even if you can but are feeling especially benevolent) instead of asking for presents, you could ask friends and family to help you to help others. They could:

- Make a donation to a cause you care about.

- Sponsor you to take part in a charity event.

- Buy a 'good gift' for someone in a developing country, such as chickens, goats, or mosquito nets.

- Buy a restaurant voucher for a family who can't afford to eat out together.

- Give you a gift you'd like to re-gift to someone else. (with the buyer's blessing.)

'Kindness is always fashionable and always welcome.'

Amelia Barr

KINDNESS AT
Christmas

- Invite someone who would otherwise be on their own to share your Christmas meal.

- Prepare gift bags for elderly people.

- Volunteer in a hostel.

- Make festive decorations for other people.

- Buy gifts for children in hospital.

- Send care packages to servicemen and women.

- Gather a group of friends or children together and sing carols in the street, or outside care homes.

- Hand out candy canes.

- Buy socks, hats, blankets, or other useful items for people who are homeless.

REVERSE ADVENT CALENDAR

This is a fun and simple way to practise kindness at Christmas with a calendar that gives something back. The idea is to take an empty box and put one item into it every day between December 1st and December 24th, to mirror the traditional advent calendar. When the box is full, take it to a charity or food bank, or even donate it to someone you know facing hardship at Christmas.

Your reverse advent calendar could include non-perishable foods, toiletries, toys for children living in poverty, treats, and anything else you can think of.

'If you want to be a rebel, be kind.'

Pancho Ramos Stierle

NEW YEAR
KINDNESS RESOLUTIONS

Why not make a list of all your kindness resolutions?
They could have been inspired by this book, or
perhaps you have some ideas of your own. Don't
forget to make a note of the outcome, too. Of course,
you don't need to wait until January – kindness is
always in season and the results will last a lifetime.
Happy New Kindness Year!

'Do your little
bit of good where
you are; it's those
little bits of good
put together that
overwhelm the world.'

Desmond Tutu

'This is my simple religion. There is no need for temples; no need for complicated philosophy. Our own brain, our own heart is our temple; the philosophy is kindness.'

Dalai Lama

If you have finished with this book, why not pass it on to someone else and keep the wheels of kindness in motion.